You're Never Too Old for Nuts and Berries

Doonesbury books by G.B. Trudeau

In Large Format

a Doonesbury classic by

GB Trudeau.

You're Never Too Old
for Nuts and Berries

An Owl Book   Holt, Rinehart and Winston / New York

Published by Holt, Rinehart and Winston, 383 Madison Avenue,
New York, New York 10017.

Published simultaneously in Canada by Holt, Rinehart and
Winston of Canada, Limited.

Library of Congress Catalog Card Number: 76-6751

ISBN: 0-03-018216-6

Printed in the United States of America

The cartoons in this book have appeared in newspapers
in the United States and abroad under the auspices of
Universal Press Syndicate.

10 9 8 7 6

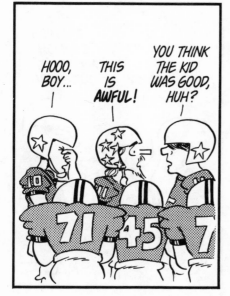

FIRST, A BRIEF RATIONALE FOR THIS COURSE. HEAR ME OUT.

AMBROSE BIERCE ONCE DEFINED A LAWYER AS "ONE SKILLED IN CIRCUMVENTING THE LAW." IT WAS A DEVIL'S DEFINITION, OF COURSE, BUT THE EVENTS OF RECENT YEARS HAVE MORE THAN ONCE LENT IT TRUTH.

IT IS NOT SUFFICIENT FOR A LAWYER TO SIMPLY **KNOW** THE LAW. LAW SCHOOLS TODAY HAVE A FAR MORE FUNDAMENTAL OBLIGATION TO INSURE THAT THEIR GRADUATES HAVE AN UNDERSTANDING OF ITS **SPIRIT,** ITS **MORAL ESSENCE!**

"RIGHT AND WRONG 10-A" IS ONE SUCH STAB IN THE DARK.

GBTrudeau

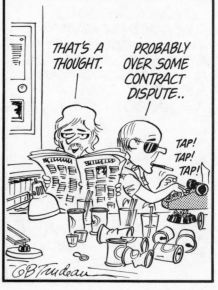

"AND SO WITH VOWS OF MUTUAL RESPECT, NATE AND AMY'S RECONCILIATION WAS ASSURED..."

BOTH HAD LEARNED MUCH ABOUT THEMSELVES IN AMY'S ABSENCE. WHILE THEIR LOVE HAD NEVER BEEN IN QUESTION, THEIR PERSONAL STRENGTHS AND LIMITATIONS WERE NOW FAR MORE CLEAR TO THEM..

EXCUSE ME, MIKE... I HAVE A CALL TO MAKE..

GOOD LUCK, SIR.

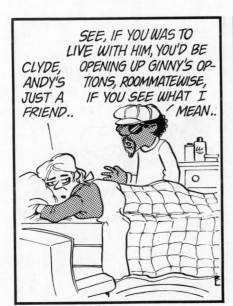